this planner
belongs to

....

....

contact

....

....

About the artist

MEERA LEE PATEL

Meera Lee Patel is a self-taught artist and the internationally best-selling author of several books on mental and emotional health, including *How It Feels to Find Yourself: Navigating Life's Changes with Purpose, Clarity, and Heart*. Her journals include *Start Where You Are*, a journal for self-exploration, and the upcoming *Go Your Own Way*, a journal for building self-confidence.

Meera creates work that inspires and encourages others to connect with themselves, each other, and the world around them. Her signature watercolor paintings are known for their vibrant, evocative feel and are traditionally paired with thoughtful passages on living a deliberate, more introspective life. Visit her at meeralee.com and follow her on Instagram @meeraleepatel.

Describe three ways you've grown over the past year.

_____
_____
_____
_____
_____
_____
_____
_____
_____
_____
_____
_____
_____
_____
_____
_____

2024 AT A GLANCE

JANUARY 2024

S	M	T	W	T	F	S
	1	2	3	4	5	6
7	8	9	10	11	12	13
14	15	16	17	18	19	20
21	22	23	24	25	26	27
28	29	30	31			

FEBRUARY 2024

S	M	T	W	T	F	S
				1	2	3
4	5	6	7	8	9	10
11	12	13	14	15	16	17
18	19	20	21	22	23	24
25	26	27	28	29		

MARCH 2024

S	M	T	W	T	F	S
					1	2
3	4	5	6	7	8	9
10	11	12	13	14	15	16
17	18	19	20	21	22	23
24	25	26	27	28	29	30
31						

APRIL 2024

S	M	T	W	T	F	S
	1	2	3	4	5	6
7	8	9	10	11	12	13
14	15	16	17	18	19	20
21	22	23	24	25	26	27
28	29	30				

MAY 2024

S	M	T	W	T	F	S
			1	2	3	4
5	6	7	8	9	10	11
12	13	14	15	16	17	18
19	20	21	22	23	24	25
26	27	28	29	30	31	

JUNE 2024

S	M	T	W	T	F	S
						1
2	3	4	5	6	7	8
9	10	11	12	13	14	15
16	17	18	19	20	21	22
23	24	25	26	27	28	29
30						

JULY 2024

S	M	T	W	T	F	S
	1	2	3	4	5	6
7	8	9	10	11	12	13
14	15	16	17	18	19	20
21	22	23	24	25	26	27
28	29	30	31			

AUGUST 2024

S	M	T	W	T	F	S
				1	2	3
4	5	6	7	8	9	10
11	12	13	14	15	16	17
18	19	20	21	22	23	24
25	26	27	28	29	30	31

SEPTEMBER 2024

S	M	T	W	T	F	S
1	2	3	4	5	6	7
8	9	10	11	12	13	14
15	16	17	18	19	20	21
22	23	24	25	26	27	28
29	30					

OCTOBER 2024

S	M	T	W	T	F	S
		1	2	3	4	5
6	7	8	9	10	11	12
13	14	15	16	17	18	19
20	21	22	23	24	25	26
27	28	29	30	31		

NOVEMBER 2024

S	M	T	W	T	F	S
					1	2
3	4	5	6	7	8	9
10	11	12	13	14	15	16
17	18	19	20	21	22	23
24	25	26	27	28	29	30

DECEMBER 2024

S	M	T	W	T	F	S
1	2	3	4	5	6	7
8	9	10	11	12	13	14
15	16	17	18	19	20	21
22	23	24	25	26	27	28
29	30	31				

HOLIDAYS

The holidays listed in this calendar are accurate to the best of our knowledge and research. All times are given in Eastern Standard Time (EST), which is noted as Eastern Daylight Time (EDT) during Daylight Saving Time.

The Islamic calendar is based on lunar observation and thus may vary depending upon the sighting of the crescent moon. Dates apply to North America.

Solar and lunar eclipses are not viewable from all regions.

JANUARY 2024
1 New Year's Day
15 Martin Luther King Jr. Day
26 Australia Day

FEBRUARY 2024
1 Imbolc
2 Groundhog Day
6 Waitangi Day (New Zealand)
10 Lunar New Year (Dragon)
13 Mardi Gras
14 Ash Wednesday, Lent begins
14 Valentine's Day
15 Flag Day (Canada)
17 Random Acts of Kindness Day
19 Presidents' Day
29 Leap Day

MARCH 2024
8 International Women's Day
10 Daylight Saving Time begins
10 Mother's Day (UK)
10 Ramadan begins at sunset
17 St. Patrick's Day
19 Spring Equinox
29 Good Friday
31 British Summer Time begins (UK)
31 Easter

APRIL 2024
1 April Fools' Day
1 Easter Monday (Australia, Canada, UK)
9 Eid al-Fitr begins at sunset
22 Earth Day
22 Passover begins at sunset
25 ANZAC Day (Australia, New Zealand)
26 Arbor Day

MAY 2024
1 Beltane
1 May Day
5 Cinco de Mayo
5 Pascha
6 Early May Bank Holiday (UK)
12 Mother's Day
17 Bike to Work Day
18 Armed Forces Day
20 Victoria Day (Canada, Scotland)
23 Vesak
27 Memorial Day
27 Spring Bank Holiday (UK)

JUNE 2024
5 World Environment Day
11 Shavuot begins at sunset
14 Flag Day
16 Eid al-Adha begins at sunset
16 Father's Day
19 Juneteenth
20 Summer Solstice
20 World Refugee Day

JULY 2024
1 Canada Day
4 Independence Day
6 Muharram begins at sunset
12 Orangemen's Day (Northern Ireland)

AUGUST 2024
1 Lughnasadh
5 August Bank Holiday (Scotland)
5 Civic Holiday (Canada)
26 Summer Bank Holiday (UK)
26 Women's Equality Day

SEPTEMBER 2024
2 Labor Day (USA, Canada)
8 Grandparents Day
11 Patriot Day
21 International Day of Peace
22 Autumnal Equinox
30 National Day for Truth and Reconciliation (Canada)

OCTOBER 2024
2 Rosh Hashanah begins at sunset
11 Yom Kippur begins at sunset
14 Columbus Day
14 Indigenous Peoples Day
14 Thanksgiving (Canada)
16 Sukkot begins at sunset
24 United Nations Day
27 British Summer Time ends (UK)
31 Halloween
31 Samhain

NOVEMBER 2024
1 Diwali
3 Daylight Saving Time ends
5 Election Day
11 Remembrance Day (Australia, Canada, UK)
11 Veterans Day
28 Thanksgiving
30 St. Andrew's Day (Scotland)

DECEMBER 2024
1 Advent begins
7 Pearl Harbor Remembrance Day
10 Human Rights Day
21 Winter Solstice
25 Christmas
25 Hanukkah begins at sunset
26 Boxing Day (Australia, Canada, UK)
26 Kwanzaa begins
31 New Year's Eve

DECEMBER 2023

SUNDAY	MONDAY	TUESDAY	WEDNESDAY
26	27	28	29
3	4	◑ 12:49 am EST 5	6
10	11	● 6:32 pm EST 12	13
17	18	◑ 1:39 pm EST 19	20
24	25	○ 7:33 pm EST 26	27
31 New Year's Eve	Christmas	Boxing Day (Australia, Canada, UK) Kwanzaa begins	

  ● NEW MOON ◑ FIRST QUARTER ○ FULL MOON ◑ LAST QUARTER

THURSDAY	FRIDAY	SATURDAY
30	1	2
7	8	9
Hanukkah begins at sunset		
14	15	16
21	22	23
Winter Solstice		
28	29	30

DECEMBER

What do you wish most for yourself in the new year?

DECEMBER 2023

FRIDAY

1

SATURDAY

2

SUNDAY

3

Advent begins

MONDAY

4

TUESDAY

5

◑ 12:49 am EST

WEDNESDAY

6

7

Hanukkah begins at sunset | Pearl Harbor Remembrance Day

8

9

10

Human Rights Day

MONDAY

11

TUESDAY

12

● 6:32 pm EST

WEDNESDAY

13

Mercury retrograde until January 1

THURSDAY

14

FRIDAY

15

SATURDAY

16

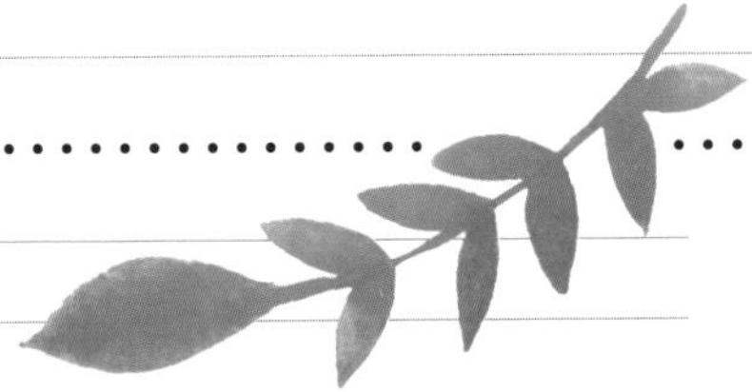

SUNDAY

17

MONDAY

18

TUESDAY

19

◐ 1:39 pm EST

WEDNESDAY

20

THURSDAY

21

Winter Solstice 10:28 pm EST

FRIDAY

22

SATURDAY

23

SUNDAY

24

MONDAY

25

Christmas

TUESDAY

26

Boxing Day (Australia, Canada, UK) | Kwanzaa begins | ○ 7:33 pm EST

WEDNESDAY

27

28

FRIDAY
29

SATURDAY
30

SUNDAY
31

New Year's Eve

JANUARY 2024

SUNDAY	MONDAY	TUESDAY	WEDNESDAY
31	1	2	◑ 10:30 pm EST 3
	New Year's Day		
7	8	9	10
14	15	16	◑ 10:52 pm EST 17
	Martin Luther King Jr. Day		
21	22	23	24
28	29	30	31

● NEW MOON   ◑ FIRST QUARTER   ○ FULL MOON   ◑ LAST QUARTER

THURSDAY	FRIDAY	SATURDAY
4	5	6
● 6:57 am EST 11	12	13
18	19	20
○ 12:54 pm EST 25	26	27
1	Australia Day 2	3

JANUARY 2024

MONDAY

1

New Year's Day

TUESDAY

2

WEDNESDAY

3

◑ 10:30 pm EST

FRIDAY

5

SATURDAY

6

SUNDAY

7

JANUARY 2024

MONDAY
8

TUESDAY
9

WEDNESDAY
10

● 6:57 am EST

FRIDAY

12

SATURDAY

13

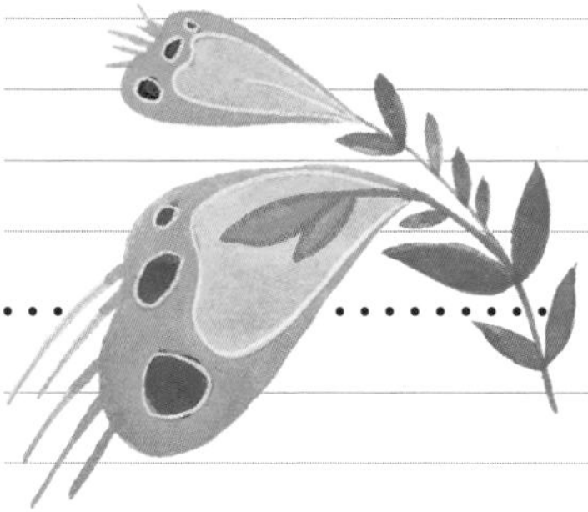

SUNDAY

14

JANUARY 2024

MONDAY

15

Martin Luther King Jr. Day

TUESDAY

16

WEDNESDAY

17

◑ 10:52 pm EST

THURSDAY
18

FRIDAY
19

SATURDAY
20

SUNDAY
21

JANUARY 2024

MONDAY

22

TUESDAY

23

WEDNESDAY

24

○ 12:54 pm EST

FRIDAY
26

Australia Day

SATURDAY
27

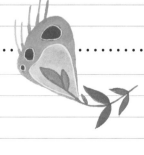

SUNDAY
28

JANUARY 2024

MONDAY

29

TUESDAY

30

WEDNESDAY

31

What is something about yourself you hope never changes?

IT IS A WONDERFUL THING
to be exactly
as you are.

MEERA LEE PATEL

FEBRUARY 2024

SUNDAY	MONDAY	TUESDAY	WEDNESDAY
28	29	30	31
4	5	6	7
11	12	13	14 Ash Wednesday, Lent begins Valentine's Day
18	19	20	21
25	26 Presidents' Day	27	28

THURSDAY	FRIDAY	SATURDAY
1	◗ 6:18 pm EST 2	3
	Groundhog Day	
8	● 5:59 pm EST 9	10
15	◖ 10:01 am EST 16	17
Flag Day (Canada)		
22	23	○ 7:30 am EST 24
29	1	2

FEBRUARY 2024

1

Imbolc

2

Groundhog Day | ◑ 6:18 pm EST

3

4

FEBRUARY 2024

MONDAY

5

TUESDAY

6

Waitangi Day (New Zealand)

WEDNESDAY

7

THURSDAY

8

FRIDAY

9

● 5:59 pm EST

SATURDAY

10

Lunar New Year (Dragon)

SUNDAY

11

FEBRUARY 2024

MONDAY

12

TUESDAY

13

Mardi Gras

WEDNESDAY

14

Ash Wednesday, Lent begins | Valentine's Day

Flag Day (Canada)

◑ 10:01 am EST

Random Acts of Kindness Day

FEBRUARY 2024

MONDAY

19

Presidents' Day

TUESDAY

20

WEDNESDAY

21

○ 7:30 am EST

FEBRUARY 2024

MONDAY

26

_____

TUESDAY

27

_____

WEDNESDAY

28

_____

Leap Day

FEBRUARY

there is beauty in BRAVERY, IN VENTURING INTO the UNKNOWN.

MEERA LEE PATEL

MARCH 2024

SUNDAY	MONDAY	TUESDAY	WEDNESDAY
25	26	27	28
◗ 10:24 am EST 3	4	5	6
● 5:00 am EDT 10 Daylight Saving Time begins Ramadan begins at sunset	11	12	13
◗ 12:11 am EDT 17 St. Patrick's Day	18	19 Spring Equinox	20
24 31 British Summer Time begins (UK) Easter	○ 3:00 am EDT 25	26	27

● NEW MOON ◗ FIRST QUARTER ○ FULL MOON ◗ LAST QUARTER

THURSDAY	FRIDAY	SATURDAY
29	1	2
7	8	9
14	15	16
21	22	23
28	29 Good Friday	30

MARCH

Write about a recent experience that required your bravery.

MARCH 2024

MARCH

◑ 10:24 am EST

MARCH 2024

MONDAY
4

TUESDAY
5

WEDNESDAY
6

International Women's Day

MARCH

Daylight Saving Time begins | Mother's Day (UK) | Ramadan begins at sunset | ● 5:00 am EDT

MARCH 2024

MONDAY

11

TUESDAY

12

WEDNESDAY

13

THURSDAY

14

FRIDAY

15

SATURDAY

16

MARCH

SUNDAY

17

St. Patrick's Day | ◑ 12:11 am EDT

MONDAY

18

_____
_____
_____
_____
_____

TUESDAY

19

_____
_____
_____
_____

Spring Equinox 11:06 pm EDT

WEDNESDAY

20

_____
_____
_____
_____
_____

THURSDAY

21

FRIDAY

22

SATURDAY

23

MARCH

SUNDAY

24

MARCH 2024

MONDAY
25

Penumbral lunar eclipse 3:13 am EDT | ○ 3:00 am EDT

TUESDAY
26

WEDNESDAY
27

FRIDAY

29

Good Friday

SATURDAY

30

SUNDAY

31

British Summer Time begins (UK) | Easter

LIFE stretches to ACCOM- MODATE YOUR VISION OF It.

MEERA LEE PATEL

APRIL 2024

SUNDAY	MONDAY	TUESDAY	WEDNESDAY
31	◑ 11:15 pm EDT 1	2	3
	April Fools' Day Easter Monday (Australia, Canada, UK)		
7	● 2:21 pm EDT 8	9	10
		Eid al-Fitr begins at sunset	
14	◐ 3:13 pm EDT 15	16	17
21	22	○ 7:49 pm EDT 23	24
	Earth Day Passover begins at sunset		
28	29	30	1

● NEW MOON   ◐ FIRST QUARTER   ○ FULL MOON   ◑ LAST QUARTER

THURSDAY	FRIDAY	SATURDAY
4	5	6
11	12	13
18	19	20
25	26	27
ANZAC Day (Australia, New Zealand)		
2	3	4

APRIL

APRIL 2024

MONDAY
1

April Fools' Day | Easter Monday (Australia, Canada, UK)
Mercury retrograde until April 25 | ◑ 11:15 pm EDT

TUESDAY
2

WEDNESDAY
3

THURSDAY

4

FRIDAY

5

SATURDAY

6

SUNDAY

7

APRIL 2024

MONDAY

8

Total solar eclipse 2:17 pm EDT | ● 2:21 pm EDT

TUESDAY

9

Eid al-Fitr begins at sunset

WEDNESDAY

10

APRIL 2024

MONDAY

15

◐ 3:13 pm EDT

TUESDAY

16

WEDNESDAY

17

THURSDAY

18

FRIDAY

19

SATURDAY

20

SUNDAY

21

APRIL 2024

MONDAY

22

Earth Day | Passover begins at sunset

TUESDAY

23

○ 7:49 pm EDT

WEDNESDAY

24

ANZAC Day (Australia, New Zealand)

Arbor Day

APRIL 2024

MONDAY
29

TUESDAY
30

What is something you'd like to accept about yourself? What are two steps you can take toward doing so?

SELf-
ACCEPtANCE
IS WELCOMING
YOURSELF
home— WHOEVER
& WHEREVER
YOU ARE.

MEERA LEE
PATEL

MAY 2024

SUNDAY	MONDAY	TUESDAY	WEDNESDAY
28 ★	29	30	◑ 7:27 am EDT 1
5	6	● 11:22 pm EDT 7	8
	Early May Bank Holiday (UK)		
12	13	14	◑ 7:48 am EDT 15
Mother's Day			
19	20	21	22
	Victoria Day (Canada, Scotland)		
26	27	28	29
	Memorial Day Spring Bank Holiday (UK)		

THURSDAY	FRIDAY	SATURDAY
2	3	4
9	10	11
16	17	18
○ 9:53 am EDT 23	24	25
◑ 1:13 pm EDT 30	31	1

MAY 2024

Beltane | May Day | ◑ 7:27 am EDT

THURSDAY

2

FRIDAY

3

SATURDAY

4

SUNDAY

5

Cinco de Mayo | Pascha

MAY 2024

MONDAY

6

Early May Bank Holiday (UK)

TUESDAY

7

● 11:22 pm EDT

WEDNESDAY

8

FRIDAY

10

SATURDAY

11

SUNDAY

12

Mother's Day

MAY 2024

MONDAY

13

TUESDAY

14

WEDNESDAY

15

☾ 7:48 am EDT

THURSDAY

16

FRIDAY

17

Bike to Work Day

SATURDAY

18

Armed Forces Day

SUNDAY

19

MAY 2024

MONDAY

20

Victoria Day (Canada, Scotland)

TUESDAY

21

WEDNESDAY

22

23

MAY

Vesak | ○ 9:53 am EDT

FRIDAY
24

SATURDAY
25

SUNDAY
26

MAY 2024

MONDAY
27

Memorial Day | Spring Bank Holiday (UK)

TUESDAY
28

WEDNESDAY
29

◑ 1:13 pm EDT

FRIDAY
31

THE MOST IMPORTANT RELATIONSHIP
WE CAN NURTURE is the ONE WE HAVE
›WITH OURSELVES.‹

MEERA LEE PATEL

JUNE 2024

SUNDAY	MONDAY	TUESDAY	WEDNESDAY
26	27	28	29
2	3	4	5
9	10	11	12
16	17	18	19
Eid al-Adha begins at sunset Father's Day			Juneteenth
23	24	25	26
30			

● NEW MOON ◐ FIRST QUARTER ○ FULL MOON ◑ LAST QUARTER

THURSDAY	FRIDAY	SATURDAY
30	31	1
● 8:38 am EDT 6	7	8
13	◑ 1:18 am EDT 14 Flag Day	15
20	○ 9:08 pm EDT 21	22
Summer Solstice 27	◑ 5:53 pm EDT 28	29

Describe three ways you are caring
for yourself physically and mentally.

JUNE 2024

SATURDAY

1

SUNDAY

2

JUNE 2024

MONDAY

3

TUESDAY

4

WEDNESDAY

5

World Environment Day

● 8:38 am EDT

JUNE

JUNE 2024

MONDAY

10

_____

TUESDAY

11

_____

Shavuot begins at sunset

WEDNESDAY

12

_____

JUNE

Flag Day | ☽ 1:18 am EDT

SATURDAY

15

SUNDAY

16

Eid al-Adha begins at sunset | Father's Day

JUNE 2024

MONDAY
17

TUESDAY
18

WEDNESDAY
19

Juneteenth

THURSDAY

20

Summer Solstice 4:51 pm EDT | World Refugee Day

FRIDAY

21

○ 9:08 pm EDT

SATURDAY

22

SUNDAY

23

JUNE 2024

MONDAY
24

TUESDAY
25

WEDNESDAY
26

JUNE

◑ 5:53 pm EDT

JULY 2024

SUNDAY	MONDAY	TUESDAY	WEDNESDAY
30	1	2	3
	Canada Day		
7	8	9	10
14	15	16	17
○ 6:17 am EDT 21	22	23	24
28	29	30	31

● NEW MOON   ◐ FIRST QUARTER   ○ FULL MOON   ◑ LAST QUARTER

THURSDAY	FRIDAY	SATURDAY
4	● 6:57 pm EDT 5	6
Independence Day		Muharram begins at sunset
11	12 ● 6:49 pm EDT 13	
	Orangemen's Day (Northern Ireland)	
18	19	20
25	26	● 10:52 pm EDT 27
1	2	3

JULY

JULY 2024

MONDAY

1

Canada Day

TUESDAY

2

WEDNESDAY

3

THURSDAY
4

Independence Day

FRIDAY
5

● 6:57 pm EDT

SATURDAY
6

Muharram begins at sunset

SUNDAY
7

MONDAY
8

TUESDAY
9

WEDNESDAY
10

Orangemen's Day (Northern Ireland)

JULY

◑ 6:49 pm EDT

MONDAY

15

_____

_____

_____

_____

_____

TUESDAY

16

_____

_____

_____

_____

_____

WEDNESDAY

17

_____

_____

_____

_____

_____

THURSDAY

18

FRIDAY

19

SATURDAY

20

SUNDAY

21

○ 6:17 am EDT

JULY 2024

MONDAY

22

TUESDAY

23

WEDNESDAY

24

THURSDAY

25

FRIDAY

26

SATURDAY

27

◑ 10:52 pm EDT

SUNDAY

28

JULY 2024

MONDAY
29

TUESDAY
30

WEDNESDAY
31

What is something you feel discouraged about? Write about it here.

CHOOSE TO KEEP TRYING

MEERA LEE PATEL

AUGUST 2024

SUNDAY	MONDAY	TUESDAY	WEDNESDAY
28	29	30	31
4 ● 7:13 am EDT	5	6	7
11	12 ◑ 11:19 am EDT August Bank Holiday (Scotland) Civic Holiday (Canada)	13	14
18	19 ○ 2:26 pm EDT	20	21
25	26 ◐ 5:26 am EDT Summer Bank Holiday (UK)	27	28

● NEW MOON   ◑ FIRST QUARTER   ○ FULL MOON   ◐ LAST QUARTER

THURSDAY	FRIDAY	SATURDAY
1	2	3
8	9	10
15	16	17
22	23	24
29	30	31

AUGUST

AUGUST 2024

Lughnasadh

Mercury retrograde until August 28 | ● 7:13 am EDT

AUGUST 2024

MONDAY
5

August Bank Holiday (Scotland) | Civic Holiday (Canada)

TUESDAY
6

WEDNESDAY
7

AUGUST 2024

MONDAY

12

◑ 11:19 am EDT

TUESDAY

13

WEDNESDAY

14

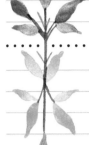

AUGUST

AUGUST 2024

MONDAY

19

○ 2:26 pm EDT

TUESDAY

20

WEDNESDAY

21

AUGUST 2024

MONDAY

26

_____
_____
_____
_____

Summer Bank Holiday (UK) | Women's Equality Day | ◑ 5:26 am EDT

TUESDAY

27

_____
_____
_____
_____

WEDNESDAY

28

_____
_____
_____
_____

AUGUST

LET YOUR OWN UNIVERSE GUIDE YOU.

MEERA LEE PATEL

SEPTEMBER 2024

SUNDAY	MONDAY	TUESDAY	WEDNESDAY
1	2 ● 9:55 pm EDT	3	4
	Labor Day (USA, Canada)		
8	9	10	11 ◐ 2:06 am EDT
15	16	17 ○ 10:34 pm EDT	18
22	23 ◐ 2:50 pm EDT	24	25
29 Autumnal Equinox	30 National Day for Truth and Reconciliation (Canada)	1	2

THURSDAY	FRIDAY	SATURDAY
5	6	7
12	13	14
19	20	21
26	27	28
3	4	5

Identify a relationship in your life
you feel resistance toward. Close your eyes
and meditate on whether this relationship
brings you joy or takes it from you.

SEPTEMBER 2024

SUNDAY

1

SEPTEMBER 2024

MONDAY
2

Labor Day (USA, Canada) | ● 9:55 pm EDT

TUESDAY
3

WEDNESDAY
4

THURSDAY

5

FRIDAY

6

SATURDAY

7

SUNDAY

8

Grandparents Day

SEPTEMBER 2024

MONDAY
9

TUESDAY
10

WEDNESDAY
11

Patriot Day | ☽ 2:06 am EDT

SEPTEMBER 2024

MONDAY

16

TUESDAY

17

Partial lunar eclipse 10:44 pm EDT | ○ 10:34 pm EDT

WEDNESDAY

18

FRIDAY
20

SATURDAY
21

International Day of Peace

SUNDAY
22

Autumnal Equinox 8:44 am EDT

SEPTEMBER 2024

MONDAY

23

TUESDAY

24

◑ 2:50 pm EDT

WEDNESDAY

25

THURSDAY
26

FRIDAY
27

SATURDAY
28

SUNDAY
29

SEPTEMBER 2024

MONDAY

30

National Day for Truth and Reconciliation (Canada)

Write about a significant change
you went through this year.
What did you learn from it?

OCTOBER 2024

SUNDAY	MONDAY	TUESDAY	WEDNESDAY
	30	1	● 2:49 pm EDT 2 Rosh Hashanah begins at sunset
6	7	8	9
13	14 Columbus Day Indigenous Peoples Day Thanksgiving (Canada)	15	16
20	21	22	23
27 British Summer Time ends (UK)	28	29	30

● NEW MOON   ◑ FIRST QUARTER   ○ FULL MOON   ◑ LAST QUARTER

THURSDAY	FRIDAY	SATURDAY	
3	4	5	
◑ 2:55 pm EDT 10	11	12	
	Yom Kippur begins at sunset		
○ 7:26 am EDT 17	18	19	
◐ 4:03 am EDT 24	25	26	
31	1	2	
Halloween			

OCTOBER 2024

TUESDAY

1

WEDNESDAY

2

Annular solar eclipse 2:45 pm EDT | Rosh Hashanah begins at sunset | ● 2:49 pm EDT

OCTOBER

OCTOBER 2024

MONDAY
7

TUESDAY
8

WEDNESDAY
9

10

◑ 2:55 pm EDT

11

OCTOBER

Yom Kippur begins at sunset

12

13

OCTOBER 2024

MONDAY

14

Columbus Day | Indigenous Peoples Day | Thanksgiving (Canada)

TUESDAY

15

WEDNESDAY

16

Sukkot begins at sunset

THURSDAY
17

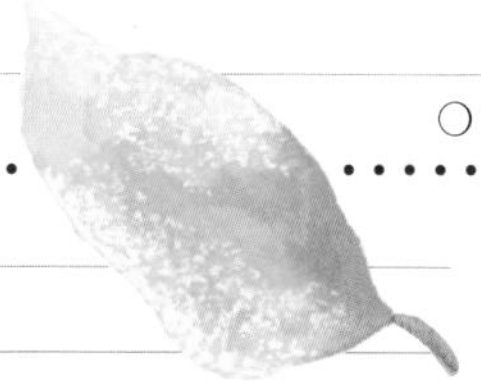

○ 7:26 am EDT
FRIDAY
18

SATURDAY
19

SUNDAY
20

OCTOBER 2024

MONDAY

21

TUESDAY

22

WEDNESDAY

23

United Nations Day | ◑ 4:03 am EDT

OCTOBER

British Summer Time ends (UK)

OCTOBER 2024

MONDAY

28

TUESDAY

29

WEDNESDAY

30

Halloween | Samhain

GO AT YOUR OWN PACE.

MEERA LEE PATEL

NOVEMBER 2024

SUNDAY	MONDAY	TUESDAY	WEDNESDAY
27	28	29	30
3 Daylight Saving Time ends	4	5 Election Day	6
10	11 Remembrance Day (Australia, Canada, UK) Veterans Day	12	13
17	18	19	20
24	25	26	27

● NEW MOON ☽ FIRST QUARTER ○ FULL MOON ☾ LAST QUARTER

THURSDAY	FRIDAY	SATURDAY
31	● 8:47 am EDT 1	2
7	8	◐ 12:56 am EST 9
14	○ 4:29 pm EST 15	16
21	◑ 8:28 pm EST 22	23
28 Thanksgiving	29	30 St. Andrew's Day (Scotland)

NOVEMBER

What is a goal you wish you could
achieve faster? What are you learning
from the journey?

NOVEMBER 2024

FRIDAY

1

Diwali | ● 8:47 am EDT

SATURDAY

2

SUNDAY

3

Daylight Saving Time ends

NOVEMBER 2024

MONDAY

4

TUESDAY

5

Election Day

WEDNESDAY

6

NOVEMBER

◐ 12:56 am EST

NOVEMBER 2024

MONDAY
11

Remembrance Day (Australia, Canada, UK) | Veterans Day

TUESDAY
12

WEDNESDAY
13

THURSDAY

14

FRIDAY

15

○ 4:29 pm EST

SATURDAY

16

SUNDAY

17

MONDAY

18

TUESDAY

19

WEDNESDAY

20

◑ 8:28 pm EST

NOVEMBER

NOVEMBER 2024

MONDAY
25

Mercury retrograde until December 15

TUESDAY
26

WEDNESDAY
27

28

Thanksgiving

29

30

St. Andrew's Day (Scotland)

NOVEMBER

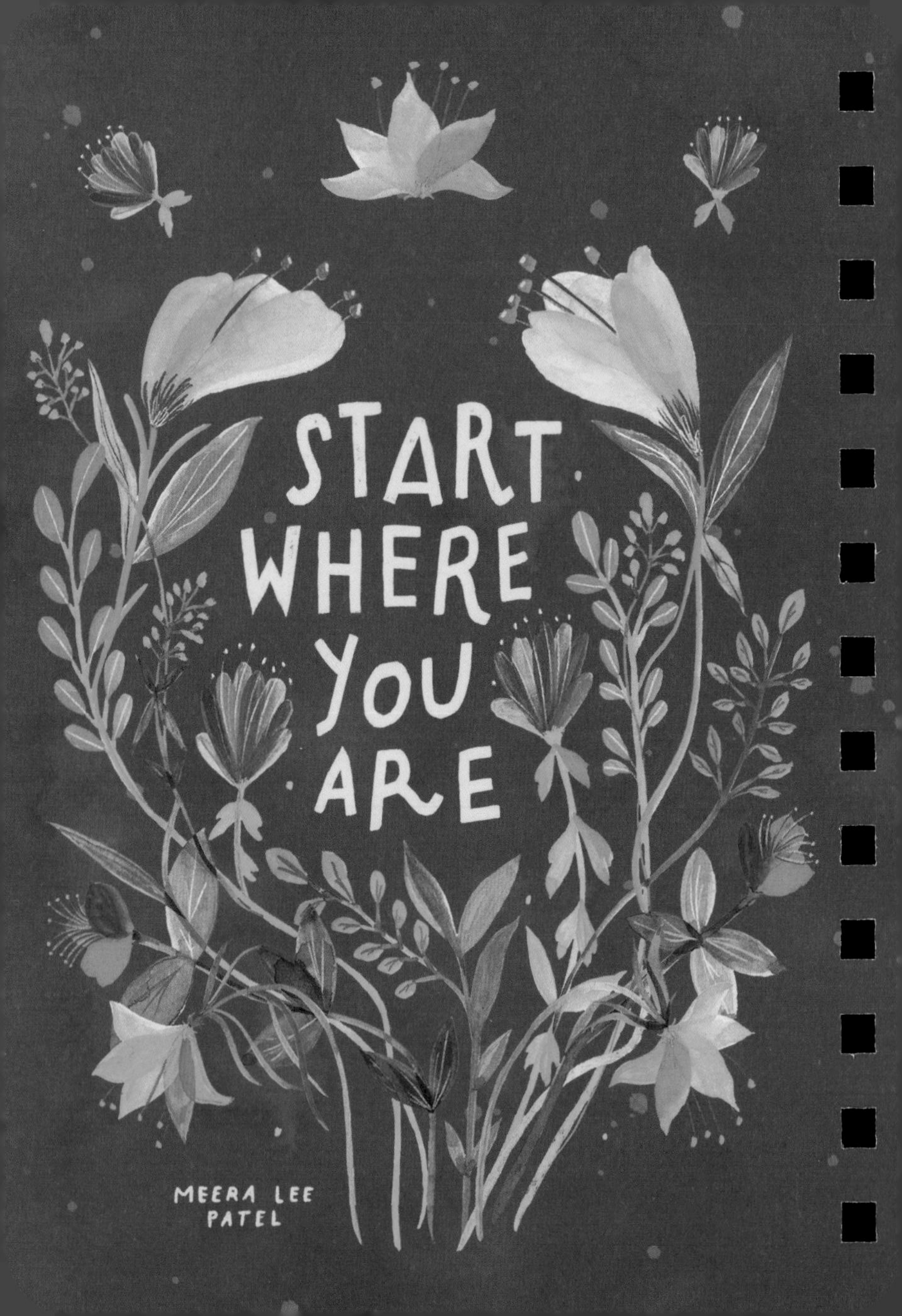
START
WHERE
YOU
ARE
MEERA LEE
PATEL

DECEMBER 2024

SUNDAY	MONDAY	TUESDAY	WEDNESDAY
● 1:21 am EST **1**	**2**	**3**	**4**
◑ 10:27 am EST **8**	**9**	**10**	**11**
○ 4:02 am EST **15**	**16**	**17**	**18**
◐ 5:18 pm EST **22**	**23**	**24**	**25** Christmas Hanukkah begins at sunset
29	● 5:27 pm EST **30**	**31** New Year's Eve	**1**

THURSDAY	FRIDAY	SATURDAY
5	6	7
12	13	14
19	20	21 Winter Solstice
26 Boxing Day (Australia, Canada, UK) Kwanzaa begins	27	28
2	3	4

Describe one way you'd like to change your life. What three steps can you take toward this?

DECEMBER 2024

SUNDAY

1

Advent begins | ● 1:21 am EST

DECEMBER 2024

MONDAY

2

TUESDAY

3

WEDNESDAY

4

Pearl Harbor Remembrance Day

DECEMBER

◗ 10:27 am EST

DECEMBER 2024

MONDAY

9

_____

_____

_____

_____

_____

_____

TUESDAY

10

_____

_____

_____

_____

_____

Human Rights Day

WEDNESDAY

11

_____

_____

_____

_____

_____

○ 4:02 am EST

DECEMBER

DECEMBER 2024

MONDAY

16

TUESDAY

17

WEDNESDAY

18

FRIDAY

20

SATURDAY

21

Winter Solstice 4:20 am EST

SUNDAY

22

DECEMBER.

◑ 5:18 pm EST

DECEMBER 2024

MONDAY

23
_____
_____
_____
_____
_____

TUESDAY

24
_____
_____
_____
_____
_____

WEDNESDAY

25
_____
_____
_____
_____

Christmas | Hanukkah begins at sunset

THURSDAY

26

Boxing Day (Australia, Canada, UK) | Kwanzaa begins

FRIDAY

27

SATURDAY

28

SUNDAY

29

DECEMBER 2024

MONDAY

30

● 5:27 pm EST

TUESDAY

31

New Year's Eve

What three values would you like to live by?

JANUARY 2025

SUNDAY	MONDAY	TUESDAY	WEDNESDAY
29	30	31	1 New Year's Day
5	◑ 6:56 pm EST 6	7	8
12	○ 5:27 pm EST 13	14	15
19	20 Martin Luther King Jr. Day	◐ 3:31 pm EST 21	22
26 Australia Day	27	28	● 7:36 am EST 29

● NEW MOON ◐ FIRST QUARTER ○ FULL MOON ◑ LAST QUARTER

THURSDAY	FRIDAY	SATURDAY
2	3	4
9	10	11
16	17	18
23	24	25
30	31	1

JANUARY 2025

WEDNESDAY

1

New Year's Day

JANUARY 2025

MONDAY

6

◑ 6:56 pm EST

TUESDAY

7

WEDNESDAY

8

THURSDAY

9

FRIDAY

10

SATURDAY

11

SUNDAY

12

MONDAY

13

○ 5:27 pm EST

TUESDAY

14

WEDNESDAY

15

THURSDAY

16

FRIDAY

17

SATURDAY

18

SUNDAY

19

JANUARY 2025

MONDAY
20

Martin Luther King Jr. Day

TUESDAY
21

◑ 3:31 pm EST

WEDNESDAY
22

THURSDAY
23

FRIDAY
24

SATURDAY
25

SUNDAY
26

Australia Day

MONDAY

27

TUESDAY

28

WEDNESDAY

29

Lunar New Year (Snake) | ● 7:36 am EST

FRIDAY

31

CONTACTS

NAME

ADDRESS

PHONE

EMAIL

NAME

ADDRESS

PHONE

EMAIL

NAME

ADDRESS

PHONE

EMAIL

NAME

ADDRESS

PHONE

EMAIL

NAME

ADDRESS

PHONE

EMAIL

CONTACTS

NAME

ADDRESS

PHONE

EMAIL

NAME

ADDRESS

PHONE

EMAIL

NAME

ADDRESS

PHONE

EMAIL

NAME

ADDRESS

PHONE

EMAIL

NAME

ADDRESS

PHONE

EMAIL

BIRTHDAYS AND OCCASIONS

JANUARY

FEBRUARY

MARCH

APRIL

MAY

JUNE

BIRTHDAYS AND OCCASIONS

JULY

AUGUST

SEPTEMBER

OCTOBER

NOVEMBER

DECEMBER

HABIT TRACKER

MONTH: _____ HABIT: _____

(1) (2) (3) (4) (5) (6) (7) (8) (9) (10) (11)

(12) (13) (14) (15) (16) (17) (18) (19) (20) (21) (22)

(23) (24) (25) (26) (27) (28) (29) (30) (31)

GOAL: _____ REWARD: _____

_____

MONTH: _____ HABIT: _____

(1) (2) (3) (4) (5) (6) (7) (8) (9) (10) (11)

(12) (13) (14) (15) (16) (17) (18) (19) (20) (21) (22)

(23) (24) (25) (26) (27) (28) (29) (30) (31)

GOAL: _____ REWARD: _____

_____

MONTH: _____ HABIT: _____

(1) (2) (3) (4) (5) (6) (7) (8) (9) (10) (11)

(12) (13) (14) (15) (16) (17) (18) (19) (20) (21) (22)

(23) (24) (25) (26) (27) (28) (29) (30) (31)

GOAL: _____ REWARD: _____

_____

HABIT TRACKER

MONTH: _____   HABIT: _____

①②③④⑤⑥⑦⑧⑨⑩⑪
⑫⑬⑭⑮⑯⑰⑱⑲⑳㉑㉒
㉓㉔㉕㉖㉗㉘㉙㉚㉛

GOAL: _____   REWARD: _____

_____

MONTH: _____   HABIT: _____

①②③④⑤⑥⑦⑧⑨⑩⑪
⑫⑬⑭⑮⑯⑰⑱⑲⑳㉑㉒
㉓㉔㉕㉖㉗㉘㉙㉚㉛

GOAL: _____   REWARD: _____

_____

MONTH: _____   HABIT: _____

①②③④⑤⑥⑦⑧⑨⑩⑪
⑫⑬⑭⑮⑯⑰⑱⑲⑳㉑㉒
㉓㉔㉕㉖㉗㉘㉙㉚㉛

GOAL: _____   REWARD: _____

_____

HABIT TRACKER

Month: _____   Habit: _____

① ② ③ ④ ⑤ ⑥ ⑦ ⑧ ⑨ ⑩ ⑪
⑫ ⑬ ⑭ ⑮ ⑯ ⑰ ⑱ ⑲ ⑳ ㉑ ㉒
㉓ ㉔ ㉕ ㉖ ㉗ ㉘ ㉙ ㉚ ㉛

Goal: _____   Reward: _____

_____

_____

Month: _____   Habit: _____

① ② ③ ④ ⑤ ⑥ ⑦ ⑧ ⑨ ⑩ ⑪
⑫ ⑬ ⑭ ⑮ ⑯ ⑰ ⑱ ⑲ ⑳ ㉑ ㉒
㉓ ㉔ ㉕ ㉖ ㉗ ㉘ ㉙ ㉚ ㉛

Goal: _____   Reward: _____

_____

_____

Month: _____   Habit: _____

① ② ③ ④ ⑤ ⑥ ⑦ ⑧ ⑨ ⑩ ⑪
⑫ ⑬ ⑭ ⑮ ⑯ ⑰ ⑱ ⑲ ⑳ ㉑ ㉒
㉓ ㉔ ㉕ ㉖ ㉗ ㉘ ㉙ ㉚ ㉛

Goal: _____   Reward: _____

_____

_____

HABIT TRACKER

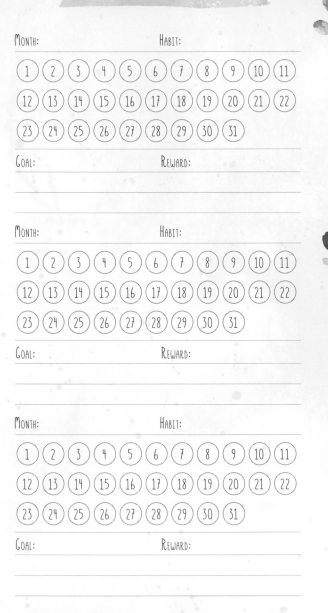

MONTH: _____ HABIT: _____

①②③④⑤⑥⑦⑧⑨⑩⑪
⑫⑬⑭⑮⑯⑰⑱⑲⑳㉑㉒
㉓㉔㉕㉖㉗㉘㉙㉚㉛

GOAL: _____ REWARD: _____

_____

MONTH: _____ HABIT: _____

①②③④⑤⑥⑦⑧⑨⑩⑪
⑫⑬⑭⑮⑯⑰⑱⑲⑳㉑㉒
㉓㉔㉕㉖㉗㉘㉙㉚㉛

GOAL: _____ REWARD: _____

_____

MONTH: _____ HABIT: _____

①②③④⑤⑥⑦⑧⑨⑩⑪
⑫⑬⑭⑮⑯⑰⑱⑲⑳㉑㉒
㉓㉔㉕㉖㉗㉘㉙㉚㉛

GOAL: _____ REWARD: _____

_____

2025 AT A GLANCE

JANUARY 2025

S	M	T	W	T	F	S
			1	2	3	4
5	6	7	8	9	10	11
12	13	14	15	16	17	18
19	20	21	22	23	24	25
26	27	28	29	30	31	

FEBRUARY 2025

S	M	T	W	T	F	S
						1
2	3	4	5	6	7	8
9	10	11	12	13	14	15
16	17	18	19	20	21	22
23	24	25	26	27	28	

MARCH 2025

S	M	T	W	T	F	S
						1
2	3	4	5	6	7	8
9	10	11	12	13	14	15
16	17	18	19	20	21	22
23	24	25	26	27	28	29
30	31					

APRIL 2025

S	M	T	W	T	F	S
		1	2	3	4	5
6	7	8	9	10	11	12
13	14	15	16	17	18	19
20	21	22	23	24	25	26
27	28	29	30			

MAY 2025

S	M	T	W	T	F	S
				1	2	3
4	5	6	7	8	9	10
11	12	13	14	15	16	17
18	19	20	21	22	23	24
25	26	27	28	29	30	31

JUNE 2025

S	M	T	W	T	F	S
1	2	3	4	5	6	7
8	9	10	11	12	13	14
15	16	17	18	19	20	21
22	23	24	25	26	27	28
29	30					

JULY 2025

S	M	T	W	T	F	S
		1	2	3	4	5
6	7	8	9	10	11	12
13	14	15	16	17	18	19
20	21	22	23	24	25	26
27	28	29	30	31		

AUGUST 2025

S	M	T	W	T	F	S
					1	2
3	4	5	6	7	8	9
10	11	12	13	14	15	16
17	18	19	20	21	22	23
24	25	26	27	28	29	30
31						

SEPTEMBER 2025

S	M	T	W	T	F	S
	1	2	3	4	5	6
7	8	9	10	11	12	13
14	15	16	17	18	19	20
21	22	23	24	25	26	27
28	29	30				

OCTOBER 2025

S	M	T	W	T	F	S
			1	2	3	4
5	6	7	8	9	10	11
12	13	14	15	16	17	18
19	20	21	22	23	24	25
26	27	28	29	30	31	

NOVEMBER 2025

S	M	T	W	T	F	S
						1
2	3	4	5	6	7	8
9	10	11	12	13	14	15
16	17	18	19	20	21	22
23	24	25	26	27	28	29
30						

DECEMBER 2025

S	M	T	W	T	F	S
	1	2	3	4	5	6
7	8	9	10	11	12	13
14	15	16	17	18	19	20
21	22	23	24	25	26	27
28	29	30	31			